Looking at Minibeasts

Butterflies and Moths

Sally Morgan

Belitha Press

Contents

Words in **bold** are explained
in the glossary on page 31.

What are butterflies and moths?

Butterflies and moths are **insects**. All insects have six legs and a body made up of three parts. Butterflies and moths have a pair of **antennae**, or feelers, on their heads. They have two pairs of wings. Some butterflies and moths have wings which are wider than your hand. Very small butterflies have wings the size of a fingernail.

All butterflies have wings, six legs and two antennae.

Butterflies and moths have large eyes. They see in colour.

This hawk-eyed moth uses its antennae to pick up smells.

Butterfly or moth?

Butterflies and moths look alike, but there are ways of telling them apart. Butterflies are usually more colourful than moths. Butterflies fly around during the day, while most moths fly at night. When a moth lands, it spreads out its wings. Most butterflies rest with their wings pressed together.

The American Moon Moth has long, feathery antennae.

A butterfly's antenna has a blob at its end. The antenna of a moth is feathery. The antenna is an insect's nose. It picks up smells in the air.

A moth (above) rests with its wings spread out. A butterfly (below) presses them together.

Butterflies have colourful wings and a blob at the end of each antenna.

Colourful wings

Butterfly wings are covered in rows of tiny **scales**. The scales overlap each other, just like tiles on a roof. When the scales catch the light

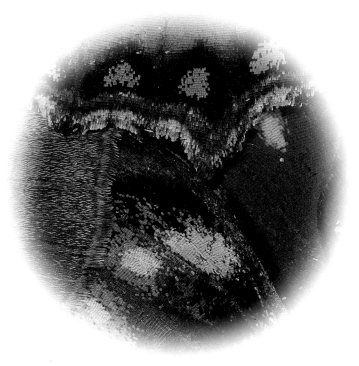

A butterfly's wing is covered in tiny scales which catch the light.

they **shimmer** with beautiful colours. Some of the most colourful butterflies live in tropical rainforests. The colours of the wings help us to identify the different butterflies and moths.

A peacock butterfly
(above) has big eye
spots on its wings.

A chalk hill blue butterfly
(below) has blue wings
with white edges.

Flying around

Butterflies and moths use their wings to fly through the air. When an insect moves its wings up and down, it is lifted into the air. Some butterflies beat their wings up to ten times every second.

The painted lady butterfly can fly across Europe.

This swallowtail butterfly moves its wings up and down to stay in the air.

Many butterflies can fly long distances.

In spring, the monarch butterfly of North

America flies hundreds of kilometres.

It travels from Mexico in the south

to Canada in the north.

*Monarch butterflies feed
on **nectar** before they
begin their long journey.*

Butterfly food

A butterfly has a long tube called a **proboscis** on its head. It uses the tube just like a drinking straw to feed on the sugary **nectar** made by flowers. The long proboscis allows the butterfly to reach deep inside the flower.

Butterflies taste food using their feet. When they land on something, they taste it. They like to eat sweet food.

In autumn, butterflies sip the juices of fallen fruit.

A butterfly (right)
sucks up nectar with
its long proboscis.

When a butterfly is
not feeding, it curls
up its proboscis
under its head.

13

What do moths eat?

Moths feed on nectar too. Moths that fly at night go to flowers that have a scent. The scent tells them that there is nectar in the flower. Hummingbird moths and bee hawk moths fly during the day. They hover beside flowers that give off a scent. Then they push their proboscis inside to drink the nectar.

The beating wings of a hummingbird moth make a humming sound.

The bee hawk moth looks like a honey bee.

The silver Y moth visits flowers during the day and at night.

Eggs and caterpillars

Butterflies and moths lay their eggs on plants.
The eggs hatch into **caterpillars**. A caterpillar
looks a bit like a worm. It has three pairs
of legs and four pairs of suckers. The legs
and suckers help the caterpillar to grip
the leaves and stems of plants.

*Caterpillars chew
leaves with their
powerful jaws.*

A large white butterfly
(*above*) lays her eggs
on cabbage leaves.

The eggs of the
large white butterfly
are yellow.

Caterpillar food

Caterpillars start eating as soon as they hatch.

They only like certain kinds of leaves.

A caterpillar eats all day. It grows so large that its skin gets tight. Then it has to **shed** the old skin and grow a larger one. Sometimes, caterpillars can kill a plant by eating all its leaves.

These buff tip moth caterpillars are eating an oak leaf.

This robin moth
caterpillar is
eating its old skin.

The privet moth
caterpillar (below)
likes to eat privet,
lilac or elder leaves.

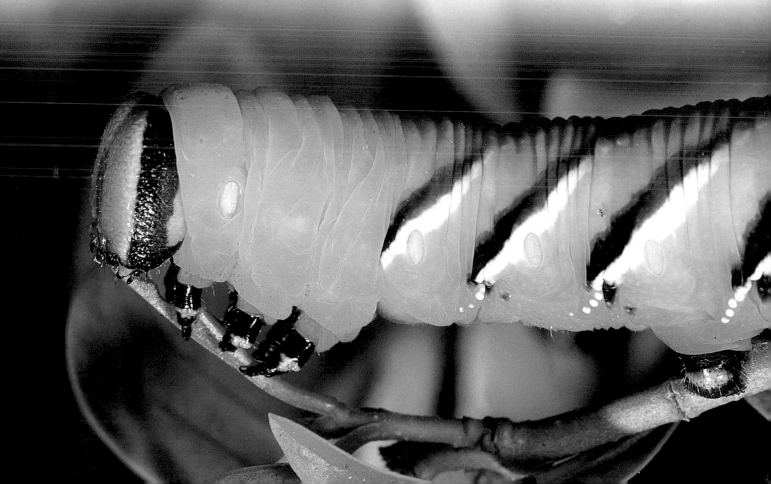

What is a pupa?

When a caterpillar is fully grown, it stops eating and sheds its skin for the last time. Lying under the old skin is a **pupa**. A pupa is a hard case made from the skin of the caterpillar.

A butterfly squeezes out of its pupa. It hangs on to the pupa while its wings harden and dry.

A new adult has to pump liquid into its wings to stretch them out.

Inside the pupa, the caterpillar slowly changes into an adult butterfly. This is called **metamorphosis**. It means changing shape. Then the pupa splits open and the new adult butterfly comes out.

Useful insects

Silk moth caterpillars feed on mulberry leaves.

Butterflies help flowers to make seeds. When a butterfly drinks nectar it becomes covered in pollen. It carries the pollen to another flower. This is called **pollination**.

The silk moth caterpillar is useful because it makes silk. When the caterpillar is fully grown it spins a type of pupa called a **cocoon**.

22

The cocoon is made of silk threads. These can be coloured and woven into a fabric called silk.

A cocoon contains about 200 metres of silk thread.

Silk fabric shimmers like a butterfly's wing.

Warning colours

Butterflies and moths have to protect themselves from animals that like to eat them. Many caterpillars have hairs, spikes or spines. Some caterpillars have eye spots to frighten away attackers. Butterflies and moths can be **poisonous** to eat. Their bright colours are a warning to other animals to stay away.

The hornet moth scares off attackers because it looks like a hornet with a nasty sting.

The hairy moth caterpillar has long hairs on its body. The hairs put off attackers.

The puss moth caterpillar rears up when it is attacked.

Colours for hiding

Many butterflies, moths and caterpillars are difficult to spot. Their colours help them to blend in with their background. This is called **camouflage**. The wings of some moths are

This green caterpillar is hiding from birds.

patterned just like the bark of a tree. Some caterpillars are shaped like twigs. This helps them to hide among the leaves of a plant.

You can hardly see the wings of this mottled beauty moth on the bark of a tree.

A *buff tip moth* (below) has wing tips that look like broken twigs.

Watching minibeasts

In summer you can see butterflies near plants that make nectar, such as lavender, poppies and buddleia. Butterflies also like to warm up on brick walls in the morning. You can see tropical butterflies and caterpillars on a butterfly farm.

Moths like to visit plants such as evening primrose and honeysuckle. You can also attract moths with sweet food. Ask a parent or teacher to help you mix up some brown sugar, ripe fruit and warm water. Paint the runny mixture on to a tree for the moths to feed on at night.

Use a paintbrush to paint the moth food on to the trunk of a tree.

At night, moths fly towards a bright light such as a torch.

To watch moths at night, ask a parent to hang up a white sheet. When you shine a torch through the sheet, moths will fly towards the light. Their outlines appear on the sheet.

You often find caterpillars near nettles. They can be kept in a fish tank for a few days, with plenty of fresh leaves to eat. Always put the caterpillars back where you found them.

Large white caterpillars eat cabbage leaves.

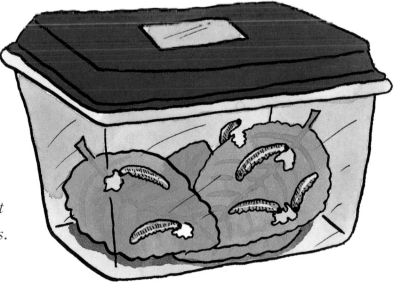

Minibeast sizes

Butterflies and moths come in many sizes. The pictures in this book do not show them at their actual size. Below you can see how big they are in real life.

Chalk hill blue butterfly
40 millimetres wide

Peacock butterfly
70 millimetres wide

Bee hawk moth
55 millimetres wide

Mottled beauty moth
45 millimetres wide

Glossary

antennae The feelers on an insect's head.

camouflage How an animal uses its colours to hide.

caterpillar The larva of a butterfly or moth.

cocoon A silk case made by a caterpillar.

insect An animal with six legs and three parts to its body.

metamorphosis When a young insect changes into an adult insect.

nectar Sugary liquid made by flowers.

poisonous Harmful.

pollination When an animal carries pollen from one flower to another. The flower can then make seeds.

proboscis The feeding tube on the head of an insect.

pupa A hard case made from the skin of a larva.

scale A tiny flake on the wing of a butterfly or moth.

shed To get rid of something naturally, such as skin or hair.

shimmer To shine with moving light.

Index

Editor: Russell McLean
Designers: John Jamieson, Ian Butterworth
Picture researcher: Sally Morgan
Educational consultant: Emma Harvey

First published in the UK in 2000 by
Belitha Press
A member of Chrysalis Books plc
64 Brewery Road, London N7 9NT

Paperback edition first published in 2002

ISBN 1 84138 165 9 (hardback)
ISBN 1 84138 389 9 (paperback)

Printed in Hong Kong

British Library Cataloguing in Publication Data
for this book is available from the British Library.

10 9 8 7 6 5 4 3   (hardback)
10 9 8 7 6 5 4 3 2 1 (paperback)

Picture acknowledgements:
Frank Blackburn/Ecoscene: front cover c, 8, 10c.
Ecoscene: 19t. Sally Morgan/Ecoscene: 23b. Papilio:
front & back cover tl, tcl, tr; front cover b, 2b, 3b, 5t,
5b, 7c, 9t, 13, 15t, 19b, 20bl, 20br, 21, 22, 23t, 24, 25, 27b,
30cr, 30bl. Jean Preston-Mafham/Premaphotos: front &
back cover tcr, 11b. Ken Preston-Mafham/Premaphotos:
4, 7t, 13t, 14, 15b, 16, 17t, 18, 25t, 26, 27t, 30br.
Rod Preston-Mafham/Premaphotos: 3t, 7b, 12, 17b.
Barrie Watts: 6, 10bl, 10br.
Robin Williams/Ecoscene: 1, 2t, 9b, 30cl.